MAGIC refrigerator

Sent Me to Paris Free

7 Rules

to

Make Dreams Come True

by
Lolly Anderson

*Jennifer —
May your dreams come true!
Lolly*

ISBN 978-0-939965-39-7

Published by

MACEDON

Cover design by Matt Goad
www.thehitshow.com

~ Contents ~

Accepting the unacceptable transforms and opens up whole new horizons.

COROLLARY: Forgiveness accepts the unacceptable in ourselves and others creating powerful transformation.

What we think about is what we get. We are always moving toward our most dominant thought, whatever it is.

COROLLARY: We can attract what we desire by thinking about its reality in our life instead of focusing on the obstacles.

Operating out of a place of trust, rather than fear, allows miraculous results.

COROLLARY: Faith is the ultimate paradox. It asks us to do something completely counterintuitive and yet is the most dependable action we will ever take.

Every problem in the world, personal or global, has a balance issue.

COROLLARY: Incremental balancing on the physical, intellectual, and spiritual planes brings exponential results.

*T*his is not based on a true story. It *is* a true story. I went to Paris and came back on the Concorde free. I was hired in several jobs for the salary I desired. After several failed relationships, I am married to the love of my life and doing what I love to do.

My life was transformed by following seven rules that I created out of my crucibles and triumphs—and by posting my heart's desires on my refrigerator. This book is the story of my transformation.

During this transformation, I discovered universal principles that helped (and still help) me fulfill my dreams. These 7 Rules will help your dreams come true.

LOLLY ANDERSON
2006

✣ 1 ✣
Acceptance

1ST RULE OF THE UNIVERSE
Accepting the unacceptable
transforms and opens up
whole new horizons.

COROLLARY:
Forgiveness accepts the
unacceptable in ourselves
and others creating powerful
transformation.

*S*omehow we wake up with this idea that loss is not supposed to happen to us. When we do experience loss, we go through all kinds of gyrations—(what did I do to deserve this? I never thought it would happen to me)—anything but accept the loss as part of life. We lose loved ones, body parts, jobs, houses, our youth, our health. All of us eventually lose our breath and die. Picture a high-profile female professional, divorced, just about to turn 50. She lands a great job with PBS, the Public Broadcasting Service, and rents an apartment in a high-rise just across the Potomac River from Washington, D.C.

Three months later, she is diagnosed with breast cancer. Each visit to the doctor brought more bad news. Retail therapy was her coping mechanism. She would buy, with her credit card, an imported rug, antique silver, or a cashmere sweater. Years ago at a party, her good friend Skipper Jones described her as having "a magnetic personality: everything she has on is charged!" That description fit her in the days of her cancer treatment more than it ever did.

She undergoes a lumpectomy. Thinking she would have an implant popped in to make her bodice symmetrical again, she discovers that reconstructive surgery is possible only if the entire breast is removed.

"Well, at least you're alive," her gynecologist told her when she lamented about her scarred half breast. "Death is not the issue! It's disfigurement!" she screamed. For someone who played in her mother's lingerie drawers, losing half a breast was a huge issue. Losing the entire breast including the nipple was catastrophic.

But it was that or live the rest of her life visibly asymmetrical with a withered, scarred misshaped breast. The fact that she was single added to her devastation. The protocol follow-up treatment to a lumpectomy—radiation—makes the tissue tougher, smaller and darker, and reconstructive surgery impossible. The tattoo graph that is applied for the benefit of the radiology technician would mark her further.

Along with the trauma of losing all the breast tissue on her right side, she was faced with the decision of what kind of reconstructive surgery to choose. There are many options, all of them irreversible. Should she choose the one where tissue from her abdomen is tunneled up to make a breast? Or the one that leaves a scar in her back from pulling a muscle around to the front to create a breast-shaped object?

After many tears, bottles of red wine, medical consultations, and prayers, she finally accepts the unacceptable about that situation. After all, her chances of survival improve a few percentage points with aggressive surgery, and she will be symmetrical again, she thinks.

She chooses saline implants. (Saline implants give her back all her tears.) The general surgeon will remove all her breast tissue and then the plastic surgeon immediately will insert a "tissue expander" so that the skin that is left can be stretched by saline injections every week over the next three months.

On the job the day before she is to check in at the hospital for the mastectomy, her assistant (a woman she had hired) hands her a two-page letter explaining how their relationship needs to improve, how she isn't a good manager, how the assistant isn't included enough in decision making. "You will have downtime to think," the assistant explained. And to top it off, the assistant copied the letter to her boss' boss. "How incredibly insensitive," thought the professional. "How unacceptable," said her inner voice. She didn't sleep a wink the night before her surgery.

She turns 50. Her closest friend, Gail Chapman Haynes, throws a Veuve Clicquot champagne party for her at the Morrison House in Alexandria, Virginia. The tissue expander in her body had grown bigger and bigger with the saline injections. Symmetry to her body goes grotesquely in the opposite direction. She wears a loose blouse and a scarf to hide her bodice.

After her third surgery for the saline implant, she goes to the hospital once again for the nipple reconstruction. Her new nipple looks like a skin flap. The tattoo procedure done later to color her new nipple was so painful she was soaked with perspiration. She endures the pain and cost again for another tattoo to get color symmetry. (She had no idea that in four years the implant would break and she would have to go through the entire set of procedures again.)

Twenty-four months later the new CEO of PBS orders a 20 percent downsizing. Employees whisper about layoffs behind closed doors, but (as they would tell her later) no one thought this well-liked woman would be in the numbers. After all, PBS gave her a performance bonus her first two years.

But the unimaginable, unacceptable happens. She's part of a reduction-in-force (a nice way of saying "you're fired"). And that is a scary situation when you have no trust fund or liquid savings to fall back on and you live in the expensive Washington, D.C. area.

On the very same day she lost her job at PBS (March 15th, the Ides of March), her gynecologist tells her that her latest uterine sonogram looks suspicious. A fourth surgery is necessary to make sure she does not have endometrial cancer caused by the tamoxifen prescribed to prevent breast cancer recurrence.

You know who that woman is.

In the midst of these crises, I called my former church in Oklahoma City to order the senior minister's taped sermons, which I had ordered from time to time through the years.

The church secretary told me that the minister had retired ("He's too young to retire," I thought) and that his wife had died. "I am so terribly sorry. I'd like to write a note. What is his address?" The secretary told me: "Don't write. Call. Let me give you his number."

Little did I know that at one of the worst times in my life, a new door was about to open. I will tell the remarkable story of what happened in a later chapter.

Like so many other times in my life, I searched for spiritual passages to get me through my crisis with breast cancer and unemployment. Living on my refrigerator along side my dreams and goals, helping me during this difficult time, were comforting passages like this one, from my mother's church bulletin:

> *When thro' fiery trials thy pathway shall lie,*
> *My grace all sufficient shall be thy supply.*
> *The flames shall not hurt thee, I only design*
> *Thy dross to consume and thy gold to refine.*

These experiences in the late 1990s, although catastrophic for me then, are not worse than what others go through. But loss is cumulative in our memory, and loss opens up old wounds.

I always dreamed of marriage, lasting love, children, and yes, money. In my twenties I was married, divorced, and then within four years married and divorced a second time. It was an incredibly painful time for me. Later, I married a third time, but that too ended in divorce after a much longer time and with unimaginable financial consequences for me and my former husband.

In my first marriage I learned about different ways individuals express love and remorse. To apologize, my lawyer husband had given me jewelry, but that wasn't good enough for me. I wanted my husband to *say* he was sorry. I judged his way of expressing his feelings as being inferior to my way.

Pain, however, can cause us to move in new directions. My dashed dream of having a family prompted me to go to law school. Working all day and taking classes at night for three years was drudgery, and a law degree is not an even trade for having children. Still, I am grateful for the intellectual and financial benefits.

If we believed that every second of suffering has meaning in our life, wouldn't we view it differently? If we understood that every experience prepares us to do our life's work, would we not accept it more peacefully? We can learn so much from the bumps in the road. Our journey is rich with exquisite lessons, and there's nothing like pain to get our attention.

Naturally we want painful situations to end as soon as possible. We want our goals to quickly come to fruition. But everything has a process and each of us is a work of art. Like other works of art, we cannot circumvent the creative process.

It may take years to learn all the lessons an experience presents, and that certainly has been true of my second marriage and divorce. The financial settlement was unfair, and I still have a way to go to completely forgive myself and my former husband, with whom I have had no contact in more than 25 years.

All along the way his family, who had tremendous wealth, made sure to preserve it for themselves. I clung to my grandfather's assessment of that situation who said, "That man has no honor." My former husband's grandmother even stated, "I thought it was awful what happened, but my hands were tied." The advice of another person was more helpful: "Resentment," she said, "is like giving yourself poison and expecting the other person to die."

The real eat-your-insides anger I harbored for years about my second divorce was anger toward myself for not fighting for a fair settlement. When this person I was in love with announced to his mother we were engaged, she said, "She is marrying you for your money." He responded, "No, Mother, just because you married for money doesn't mean Lolly is." (A curious statement since my future mother-in-law had her own multi-million dollar trust fund.)

During the divorce, I allowed her false accusation at the time of my engagement to her son to cloud my judgment. I was declaring to the world, "I don't need their name or money," but I went overboard.

Was I trying out for "Designer Doormat" or just naïve to expect, in this case, an equitable division without going to court? And was it the actual dollar amount that bothered me, or that I felt they valued money and possessions more than me?

My feelings were electrocuted. I clung to a book by photographer Dewitt Jones and editor

Eleanor Huggins, *What the Road Passes By*, because of its poignant and relevant passages, selected by Huggins, and its "achingly beautiful" photographs by Jones. My favorite quotation in the book is this one by Richard Caniell, well known in the music world for his extraordinary operatic restorations:

> *There are parched and barren fields in our lives. There is autumn in our existence. But these are the grounds of our growth, the seedbeds of our miracles. In these fields, we will someday blossom, and the innocence of the world will return with our own.*

The innocence of the world did return with my own: after memorizing and quoting this passage to my friends for years, I then read it at my wedding in 2003.

The message in *What the Road Passes By* is clear. From Dag Hammarskjöld to Dewitt Jones, Richard Caniell, and others, we are asked to experience our pain and suffering in a larger context, to listen to the world "as if it were music…because it is."

Now I am beginning to accept that I, like everyone else, sometimes use poor judgment, make mistakes, and perform at less than my best. Successful people in this world learn from their missteps, whether personal or professional. Many successful people laugh at themselves and then move on. They don't take themselves so seriously.

No one is perfect. No *thing* is perfect. When fear creeps in, instead of just *being* ourselves (because that is enough), we become fanatical for a perfect house, a perfect wardrobe, a perfect work-product, a perfect spouse. Everything outside of us takes on enormous importance when we haven't spent enough time on the inside. When I am in a panic over material things, it's a signal that my priorities are out of line.

This is not to say that striving for excellence is undesirable. But excellence is different from perfectionism. Excellence comes from passion; perfectionism comes from fear.

Fascinating people are not known for

their perfect *anything*, except perhaps for being perfectly themselves. Imperfections and vulnerabilities create subtle characteristics that endear us to others. Often what we perceive as our weaknesses are our strengths in disguise.

I have been criticized for being too open with my thoughts and feelings, and yet it is that openness which is essential for a writer. Others may judge my life experiences (and my mistakes) as a reflection of my character. Yet my crucibles have opened doors of understanding that connect me to other people.

The meaning we attach to pain determines how we process it. I have not experienced the pain of childbirth, but every mother will tell you the pain was worth it. The pain, both emotional and physical, I experienced after breast surgery takes its minor place viewed from the perspective that the surgery saved my life.

Like surgeons, we can cut away the malignant tumors in our psyches, that negative self-talk that robs us of our life.

I cannot conclude this chapter without mentioning the worst, most painful loss of all—the death of a loved one. That loss can be paralyzing, and it is excruciating when we feel we did not fully express our love for that person.

When my father died suddenly of a heart attack at age 66, I had deep regret that I failed so many times to show him my love. Daddy, who was a U.S. Air Force pilot, spent a year in Vietnam in 1968. In his letters which I still have, he implored, "Please write me." But I wrote only a few times.

Years later he and my mother were returning from a cruise and had a layover in Dallas, where I was living with my third husband. Daddy called to ask me to meet them for a short visit at the airport. I told him I would be there, but then I let my husband convince me not to go. Daddy waited for me outside the terminal thinking I would be driving up any second. I regret not doing what I thought was the right thing to do.

I wish I could write those letters; I wish I could go to the airport. I cannot go back, but I can tell others how much I loved my father. My heart hurts to write this. Today, am I showing those I love how much I care for them?

Misfortunes one can endure—they come from outside, they are accidents. But to suffer for one's own faults—ah!—there is the sting of life!
Oscar Wilde's *Lady Windermere's Fan*

God did give my family a gift before Daddy died. On the morning of his death he told my mother about a dream he had the night before. He said, "I saw confusion and chaos everywhere, but I could take my hands and part that chaos like a curtain. And everything behind the curtain was *beautiful*." Daddy died nine hours later.

Forgiveness is at the core of Christianity, and forgiveness is why one year of one person's life over 2,000 years ago still creates the power of acceptance in the 21ˢᵗ century. In the Gospel of Mark, that person—Jesus—says, "What things soever ye desire, when ye pray, believe that ye receive them, and ye shall have them." This passage immediately precedes the verse about forgiveness.

Jesus talks about forgiving others (and about God forgiving us after we have forgiven others) but Jesus does not mention forgiving oneself. My interpretation is that in the state of unforgiveness, that is, before we forgive ourselves, we *are* "other" for we are not at one with ourselves.

If only we could internalize Paul Tillich's immensely comforting words: *You are accepted, accepted by that which is greater than you. Do not try to do anything now; perhaps later you will do much. Do not seek for anything; do not perform anything; do not intend anything. Simply accept the fact that you are accepted. Sometimes it happens that we receive the power to say 'yes' to ourselves, grace has come upon us.*

We can break free from our prisons of hurt, inadequacy, regret, and fear by accepting the unacceptable and by forgiving. Forgiveness, whether it is forgiving ourselves or forgiving someone else, is the most powerful action in human existence: we move on to the next great miracle rather than hold ourselves down in a negative morass. Forgiving others as God forgives us lays the foundation for the transformation of our lives and empowers us to co-create with the universe.

The priest in Victor Hugo's *Les Miserables*

forgives Jean Valjean for stealing the only thing of value the priest had: his silver candlesticks. That act of forgiveness changes Valjean's life. The priest's act of love is so powerful that Valjean becomes capable of sacrificial love.

Accepting the unacceptable is the hardest of the 7 Rules. Paradoxically, following the rule lifts us out of the abyss of regret and remorse and brings us peace. Accepting the unacceptable unblocks our energy so that we can map out our dreams. Acceptance removes the chalks from our wheels so we can take off and fly. It lets go of the baggage that weighs us down. Accepting the unacceptable is not letting the past dictate the future.

How do we accept the unacceptable? Begin by realizing that unacceptable things happen to of all us. Accept lessons in life with humility and faith. Think about a good friend who is undergoing chemotherapy for cancer or someone like Helen Keller, who never let her blindness or deafness limit her. Choose to forgive yourself and others. Take off the judge's robe. You will be amazed at the transformation that takes place.

THE ULTIMATE COCKTAIL
DAILY AFFIRMATIONS FOR ACCEPTANCE

Today I transform my self
and world by accepting the
unacceptable.

Today I shower forgiveness on
everyone including myself.

Today I experience joy instead of
judging.

Today I accept people and
situations exactly as they are.

Today I look for meaning in pain,
suffering, and loss.

Today I believe the truth that I am
accepted by God.

Today my heart changes in the
mystery and paradox of love.

Additional passages that help me
accept the unacceptable:

*Every word and act of Jesus in the Bible reflects
these two truths: first, the Kingdom of God is in
you, and second, every person needs forgiveness.
If we work on these two premises, we will find the
renewing spirit of God in our lives. It will change
everything. It is a new reality. It is a new world.*
Michael D. Anderson, *This is the Day*

*Experience is a hard teacher. It gives the test
first, and the lesson afterwards.*
Rod Talley's father, Lawton Loveall

*We can rejoice in our sufferings knowing that
suffering produces character and character
produces hope and hope does not disappoint
us because God's love has been poured into
our hearts through the Holy Spirit which has
been given to us.*
Romans 5:3-4 RSV

◦❀2❀◦
Thought

2ND RULE OF THE UNIVERSE
What we think about is what we get.
We are always moving toward our
most dominant thought,
whatever it is.

COROLLARY:
We can attract what we desire by
thinking about its reality in our life
instead of focusing
on the obstacles.

A frequent dominant thought of mine used to be eating Haagen-Daaz ice cream, and it was amazing how successful I was.

It was never a matter of thinking that I don't have the time or the money, or might have an accident on the way to the ice cream store. I just thought about how good that ice cream would taste.

And so it is with any goal or dream we may have. Whatever we want comes closer once we visualize it in our lives. If we visualize obstacles, they come. Whether you want to finish a degree, secure a certain job, marry and have children, publish a book, alleviate a world or personal problem—whatever you wish to accomplish—start by visualizing the result you want.

Your place in life, including your material environment, is determined by the thought-form you habitually hold of yourself.
Wallace Wattles, *The Science of Getting Rich and The Science of Being Great.*

I have read a library of books on the mind and motivation. Spanning a hundred years these books have a common theme: through our higher mind, we can access an energy field in the universe to create anything we want—if we don't let our lower mind block our messages.

The mind is an incredible, miraculous energy field, and yet many of us fill it with negative, useless thoughts all day, every day, instead of harnessing its vast power to help us be our best and happiest.

Carlos Castaneda explained it this way: Each of us, every day, starts with a conflict between our true mind and our daily mind, "a foreign installation." Our true mind is from our higher self and leads us in love, purpose, and hope. Our daily mind, from our lower self, is filled with worry, anxiety, and fear. Every day we have the choice to entertain our true mind or entertain our daily mind filled with foreign thoughts of negativity.

We are in charge of our thoughts. We create every one of them, yet we pretend that we can't control them. We are all too willing to let negative-thought demons into our brain and then, we don't kick them out. We put them at the head table!

I once compared these negative thoughts to sperm trying to fertilize an egg—millions of sperm—like millions of negative thoughts trying every moment to penetrate the perimeter of our mind. My husband said, "That's terrible, comparing the attack of negative thoughts to the creation of life!"

I haven't found an analogy that fits better so I will carry it one step further. We must come up with a birth control method that works. We must keep those negative-thought demons from penetrating our minds and creating a negative being that keeps growing inside us.

An analogy my husband will like better is this one. Negative thoughts stick to us like sharp burrs to our clothing when we walk through a dry field. We wouldn't think of leaving these burrs on our clothes. We pull them off. Yet we often don't pull negative thoughts out of our brains, although negative thoughts cause much more pain.

I catch myself sometimes letting negative thoughts reign supreme in my mind. I have to say to them, "Get out!" and then consciously picture myself, for example, stepping out of the cab in front of the Paris Ritz for my book signing.

This is not to say we should go through life willy-nilly pushing all serious issues to the side. It is one thing to have serious conversations with ourselves and with others regarding the world's horrendous problems (and perhaps our own problems). It is quite another matter wasting our lives worrying and fretting about events that may never happen or that we have absolutely no control over.

When I lived in McLean, Virginia, my last two years in high school (my father was stationed at the Pentagon), I remember clipping a quotation out of *Parade* magazine, which always came in the Sunday *Washington Post*. The quotation was from George Bernard Shaw and I carried it around for years: *This is the true joy in life—the being used for a purpose recognized by yourself as a mighty one; the being a force of Nature, instead of a feverish, selfish little clod of ailments and grievances complaining that the world does not devote itself to making you happy.*

With that quotation I began a lifelong practice of focusing on a certain passage, reading it over and over again, memorizing it, until another passage took its place.

Majoring in religion and philosophy in college was the perfect choice for me as I was always searching for the meaning of life. The women's college I attended, Mary Baldwin College in Staunton, Virginia, and the closest men's college, Washington & Lee University in nearby Lexington, had a program whereby a student could take a class in her major during what was called "Coed Week." I signed up for "Meaning and Existence," a class taught by one of W&L's pre-eminent philosophy professors.

This was also the week I turned 21, and (without going into too much detail), I was late when I arrived at the philosophy department building and did not know what classroom to go to. I ran into the nearest office where a professor, bespectacled, sat behind a stack of books.

"I'm looking for Meaning and Existence!" I announced frantically.

"Young lady," the professor explained as he slowly removed his glasses, "we are *all* looking for meaning and existence."

Thirty-five years later I am still searching for (and finding) meaning. Inspirational words have been my constant companions. It is still a daily struggle between my true mind and Carlos Castaneda's "foreign installation," but it easier for me now to turn that switch in my brain to the positive energy setting.

The National Cathedral in Washington hosted an extraordinary spiritual retreat where I heard Dawna Makova, author of *I Will Not Die an Unlived Life*. She urged us to tell ourselves "river stories" instead of "rut stories." Rut stories are those stories about our past or present that diminish us, all those "I'm not good enough" stories. River stories affirm our God-given talents. These are the stories that reinforce the belief that we are put on this earth for a unique purpose.

What we choose to think or feel become magnets bringing more of our nightmares or more of our dreams. You may think that idle thoughts don't matter, that dwelling on the downside is being realistic, or negative self-talk doesn't count. Nothing is further from the truth. Our subconscious minds take us seriously. So think about what you want, not about what you don't want.

We often erect barriers to our goals because we mistakenly think too much work is required. If we constantly focus on the obstacles, it *is* too much work. When we concentrate on the part we love, and keep imagining how we will feel when we reach our desired outcome, we move through the difficulties, instead of getting stuck in them.

If mothers thought first of all the risks,

expense, heartbreak, not to mention pain, of birthing and raising children, I wonder how many of us would be here right now. I used to listen to tapes by motivational coach Denis Waitley who emphasized that successful people "focus on the rewards of success, not the penalties of failure." I learned to ask myself, what would a successful outcome of my goal look like? I learned not to think (worry) about what it would be like if I failed.

But what do we do, after we reach a goal and then we discover that we need to go in another direction? It reminds me of Walt Whitman's sage conclusion that no matter what success we achieve, there will always be another challenge, another struggle. I celebrated when I was hired as an oil and gas lawyer in Dallas, and yet I came to feel deep in my soul that it was not my destination job or career.

When I was in my office at Enserch Exploration, Inc. in downtown Dallas, I would close my door and say to myself, I don't care how much money they pay me, I can't do this for the rest of my life. It sounded good—

"corporate oil and gas lawyer"— and the people at Enserch were wonderful. I wouldn't trade the experience, but it was minimally satisfying because I was externally motivated.

During that time I read articles about people at the top of their fields. Over and over I read or heard these leaders say, "I love what I do and I would do it even if I didn't get paid for it." Money was not their primary motivation. Money often followed, but it was not their driving force.

What did I love to do? I loved the fundraising I did when I was on the alumnae board of Mary Baldwin College. So I turned that volunteer job into a real job. It was wonderful to find a profession that truly suited me; however, I had to let go of my ego to make that transition. Going from corporate attorney to being annual fund director at a small women's college in Virginia drew raised eyebrows from family and friends—not accolades.

Yet it was the wisest career decision I ever made. It started me on a fast track of better jobs, increasing pay, professional fulfillment, and love for my work. I lived a rich life and loved almost every second of it. I went from force-feeding myself case law to toasting champagne glasses in fundraising. I was excited to go to work and excited to work even on weekends at fundraising events.

Naturally the professional accomplishment I am most proud of is in fundraising. When I was first hired at the University of Virginia Law School Foundation, I noticed several portraits of men in the halls of the law school but there was no evidence that any women had ever attended. I thought it would be great if the women graduates funded the renovation of the main corridor in the law school's current capital campaign. It was a $500,000 naming opportunity. My colleagues doubted the women graduates had the money or would give it.

I contacted the two women trustees and the handful of women on the alumni council. The enthusiasm was contagious. In three years I raised $1,000,000 from UVA law alumnae to create the first space in an American law school funded and named solely by women lawyers.

When Chief Justice Rehnquist gave the keynote address at the dedication of the new law grounds at UVA, he mentioned Alumnae Lobby first. (Please note the significant suffix, "ae.") When we are doing something we love to do, we have the energy to excel.

Reconnecting to my internal worth rather than chasing after external validation for the sake of ego freed me to move forward. Our ego (our small self) wants to trap us in the miserable world of materialism and position. Our higher self wants us to soar on the thermal updrafts of the creative winds that move heaven and earth. I am choosing to soar.

If we stay in touch with our higher self, our true mind, and harness the energy field available to each of us, we can forge the life we want. Or we can ignore the higher self, and let our negative thoughts, our daily mind, make the world we don't want. Our thoughts go out into the world with powerful messages.

Thoughts create events. Some we direct. Over many we have no control. Then there is a magical field that seems to work in our favor if we are clear about what we want and we don't fill our brains with fearful, negative thoughts. Think of your mind as a radio. Tune it to a clear station, not a station of static restlessness.

Passion and desire, when informed by reason and faith, put us in touch with our life's purpose. The most successful people in the world, the ones who have created something meaningful, not necessarily the ones with the most wealth, are alive with zest and purpose.

God has given each one of us a unique set of talents to use for the greater good. When we use those unique talents, love of work and passion for work are natural byproducts.

HERE'S MY RECIPE FOR MAKING A DREAM COME TRUE:

1. *Write down your dream and post it on your refrigerator.*

2. *Acknowledge that you cannot make your dream come true with your own resources.*

3. *Put faith in God and God's universe that your dream will come true according to His plan.*

4. *Visualize yourself with your dream realized every time you open the refrigerator.*

5. *Do not try to eat your way to your dream.*

Once we realize that our lives—your life, my life—are formed not by external events but by our own thoughts that act like magnets, we can create the life we most desire. And for even greater fulfillment, we can live the life we were created for—our destiny and highest good.

THE ULTIMATE COCKTAIL
DAILY AFFIRMATIONS ON THOUGHT

Today I separate my true mind from foreign thoughts of negativity.

Today I fearlessly focus on my goals and heart's desires.

Today I fill my subconscious mind with abundance and fulfillment.

Today I attract what I desire starting with my thoughts.

Today I tell myself river stories of hope, not rut stories of defeat.

Today I commit to my purpose and the universe moves in my favor.

Today my thoughts move me toward the fruition of my goals.

Additional passages help me banish negative self-talk and attract my heart's desires:

Fear turns strength into weakness. Remember that in the moment you begin to hurry you cease to be a creator and become a competitor; you drop back upon the old plane again. Whenever you find yourself hurrying, call a halt; fix your attention on the mental image of the thing you want, and begin to give thanks that you are getting it.
Wallace Wattles, *the Science of Getting Rich and the Science of Being Great.*

For I know the plans I have for you, plans to prosper you and not to harm you, plans to give you hope and a future. Then you will call upon me, pray to me, and I will listen to you. You will seek me and find me when you seek me with all your heart.
Jeremiah 29:11-13 NIV

·✿3✿·
Faith

3RD RULE OF THE UNIVERSE
Operating out of a place
of trust, rather than fear,
allows miraculous results.

COROLLARY: Faith is the
ultimate paradox. It asks us
to do something completely
counterintuitive and yet is
the most dependable action
we will ever take.

*L*ose your life to save it? Seek the Kingdom of God first and all other things will be added? Turn your life over to do God's perfect will and have more control over your life than you ever imagined? We all know what paradox means— a situation that seems self-contradictory or absurd but in reality is true. Faith is the king of paradoxes. And it is not just about an event in our lives. The third rule, Faith, is at the very core of our lives.

> *Only the paradox comes anywhere close to comprehending the fullness of life.*
> Carl G. Jung

When I was an 18-year-old college freshman, I was madly in love with Bill Ingles, a brilliant and handsome University of Virginia law student who was tragically killed in a car accident. In one horrible reality, Bill's death marked me indelibly, accelerating my spiritual quest. It was my first experience of the death of someone close.

I remember vividly my desperate effort to get to Bill's funeral in the Tidewater area of Virginia without a car or public transportation. "There is no way I can do this on my own," I said to God. "If I am supposed to be there, then You are going to have to do it." A couple of hours later, a fraternity brother of Bill called to offer me a ride. Forty years later I still visit Bill's mother, Connie, who has been and is my revered mentor.

That prayer and surrender allowing miraculous results stayed in my memory but it would be years before I practiced the faith paradox with any frequency. My moment of true surrender came, as it does for many, at the lowest point in my life. Before that defining moment—"one pierced moment whiter than the rest" as e.e. cummings might say—I considered myself religious, spiritual, a member of the "faithful." I had gone to church my entire life, had studied Christian thought at the college level, and believed I practiced Christian compassion.

But it wasn't until I found myself waking up at three in the morning that I understood for the first time that I had never really put *God* first. I had talked about it, kidded myself, but underneath I still held out.

Here I was going through my third divorce. Unthinkable (unacceptable)! My dream of a secure and happy home was shattered not only by divorce but bankruptcy as well. Living in a small town in Virginia where everyone knows everything, I went into a tailspin of shame. The bankruptcy was brought on by a string of events. My husband, Dan, and I had bought a house in Florida for his parents. When they became ill and their income (as well as some of ours) had to go to their care in nursing homes, we carried the property for a year and then sold it at a loss. Meanwhile, Dan's former employer, who had made him a partner in a limited real estate partnership, sold some of the property.

The sale of that property created a tax liability for all the partners. We couldn't pay the taxes. Our marriage continued to disintegrate and our liquid assets vanish. Dan returned to Dallas to live in our condominium there and look for a new profession.

I went to the bankruptcy hearings by myself. One more certified letter and I think I would have gone certifiably mad. I was scared to death that I would lose everything—every stick of furniture, every rug, every beautiful thing that I had acquired over the years. We had lived in a large house outside of Boston filled with expensive furniture. We had owned property in Florida and Texas, and had a high six-figure retirement nest egg. Now this. I thought of former Governor John Connolly and his wife watching as their household items—beautiful antiques—were sold at auction. Even though intellectually I understood that I was not responsible for the bankruptcy, I felt a deep humiliation to the core of my being. That is what woke me up every morning at 3 o'clock.

My conversations with God then went

something like this: "Okay, God, I haven't done such a great job with my life these forty-plus years. I'll let you take over for a while." I had been afraid if I totally gave in, surrendered to the will of God, that I would have a dull life with no luxuries. I could see myself wearing brown clothes and no makeup.

It wasn't until I said, "I turn my life over to do Your perfect will. What would You have me do today?" that really good things started happening externally and more importantly, internally, in my life. Soon after that total surrender, I was hired at the University of Virginia Law School Foundation (at exactly the salary I had posted on my magic refrigerator) and my professional career in development took off.

One can live for years sometimes without living at all, and then life comes crowding into one single hour.
Oscar Wilde in *Vera or the Nihilists*

Let's face it: we are afraid to let go of our

egos, to be vulnerable, to be controlled. But faith is *not* controlling. It is the most freeing thing in the world. We don't want to change— maybe because we are afraid of the unknown, or maybe because we think change will require too much work.

Our American money declares "In God We Trust," but do we trust God? Or do we trust the almighty dollar? We're afraid to trust God so we put our trust in Rolex, Prada, or BMW. Margaret Hunt Hill, Texas billionaire and Mary Baldwin College alumna, told me: "If you have the status, you don't need the symbol." At my most painful moments I was obsessed to surround myself with the most expensive things. I am not saying that fine objects aren't desirable. They are. What I'm saying is that I was obsessed, for example, to wear something expensive on the outside to make up for my emotional and spiritual poverty on the inside.

We think that being true to ourselves means that we must have a certain place to live, a certain car, certain clothes and jewelry, a certain attitude. Or we disdain all manifestations of wealth as a badge of honor. Underneath both facades lies an ego unwilling to surrender.

Besides buying things to cover up our fears, sometimes we feed our fears in an attempt to make them go away. In the next chapter on balance, there is more about our addictions and obsessions, which are based on fear, not faith.

If we just let go—let go of our incessant thinking and judging—we move to a higher plane, higher than we ever imagined. Remember, faith is a paradox. "No eye has seen, no ear has heard, and no mind has imagined what God has prepared for those who love him," Paul wrote in his letter to the Corinthians. We are content to be spiritually shy.

I know all this intellectually and spiritually and yet, like the daily conflict between our true mind and the "foreign installation," I fight the material/faith battle all the time. It's part of the human condition. It is the game we get to play every day.

In "Cool, Clear Water," my favorite among my Presbyterian minister husband's sermons, he talks about the reverse wells that are drilled in India. When the monsoons come, the wells fill up with water that is then pumped out during the desert drought. So with us, if we drill reverse wells, that is, if we fill our souls with the water of God, then during our desert droughts, we can depend upon the great resource of the living God to sustain us. And, the minister tells us, we all have our desert experiences: they are a gift from God.

Being afraid to trust God means we are relying on humankind's limitations and the earth's finite resources. No wonder we run around in a frantic state.

Wallace Wattles' prophetic insight written in 1910 is the precursor of most inspirational literature today:

Hurry is a manifestation of fear. Do not get in a hurry and act from superficial impulses. You can trust God for the solution of all your personal riddles. Hurry and fear will instantly cut your connection with the universal mind; you will get no power, no wisdom, and no information until you are calm.

We do get a signal when we are calm. When you want to make a decision, become really calm. Then see what happens. Every time I have done this, I will get a signal "yes, go that way," or "no, don't go that way." It works. You will know: you will feel good or bad about your decision. So many times I have said to myself, "If I had just been calmer when I made that decision I would not have made that mistake." So many times close friends have told me about their decision making, "If I had just listened to my gut!"

Another way we sabotage ourselves is being attached to outcomes, whether a solution to a problem or the realization of our goals. It's not that we give up the focus on our desires, but we give up our fear of not receiving our heart's desires. When we stay detached, we allow the right solution to emerge out of chaos and confusion, and we allow our goals to unfold in their proper time.

As my mother often told me when I was a child, "You must allow the butterfly to form within its chrysalis. You can't cut it open and make the butterfly come out. In order to fly, it must struggle to get out of the chrysalis." On my epitaph I would like this paraphrase of a Bible verse: "Take delight in the Lord, who will give you the desires of your heart, just not on your timeline." I do believe that God gives us our deepest desires, maybe not all of them and maybe not in the exact form we envisioned, and almost never as soon as we want them.

I never had children of my own, but I am now married to a man who has four grown daughters and nine grandchildren. It took me a long time to get here, but I am married to my ideal mate, my "destination husband," as he calls himself. Living in Oklahoma again was never on my radar screen. I always breathed a big sigh of relief when the plane took off from the Will Rogers Airport in Oklahoma City. Yet here I am back in Oklahoma, supremely happy. And it is not as if I feel landlocked. We live on a beautiful lake that I see right now as I write. We travel to places like Hawaii, New Zealand, and Israel. I live close to my incredible mother, a beautiful octogenarian who looks ten years younger. (She says 20.) And I am realizing one of my biggest dreams: writing and publishing this book.

Sometimes we receive supreme happiness, not what our ego desires. God prepares us first through patience, sometimes through pain. We are not the conductor of the grand symphony, let alone the composer. We play an instrument. A recent turn of events proves that once again.

My third ex-husband died in March of 2006. Dan and I were married for 12 years but were friends, albeit distant friends, for 26 years. Years ago Dan had asked me to be the executor of his will because he was estranged from his only daughter. I believed it to be a temporary situation. But the reconciliation never happened.

In shock to be in a position I never thought would happen, I performed for the first time (but not likely the last) the duties of executor. It was a huge learning experience made more painful against the backdrop of broken dreams and memories—some good, some horrendous. Dan's parting gift to me (was it an apology?) was a small life insurance policy. The confluence of past and future, loss and affirmations, stretched me spiritually to a new space.

Trusting in just our own earthbound resources is limiting. Faith in an unseen, un-provable being is counterintuitive. Yet living with the paradox of faith frees us to use the power of our minds and hearts to co-create with the almighty Creator a life beyond our wildest imagination. Our thoughts for our future are a child's crayon scribbles compared to God's grand master painting.

A PRAYER

Dear Heavenly Father,
As I face this day,
I thank you for the gift of life.
I can get so caught up in
my desires and worries
that I forget to turn my
concerns over to you.
Today I turn everything over to you
and wait patiently—
still as a glassy pond
that reflects clouds and trees—
for your images
for my life.

Amen

The Ultimate Cocktail
Daily Affirmations on Faith

Today I let in God's power to fulfill my heart's desires and purpose.

Today I listen for God's guidance in place of hurrying and worrying.

Today I release attachment to my desires to allow miraculous results.

Today I trust God's strength more than my own.

Today I step back so God can lead the way.

Today I surrender to God's plans that far exceed mine.

Today my spirit rules my mind and body.

Additional passages that help me build faith:

I said to my soul, be still. And wait without hope. For hope would be hope for the wrong thing. Wait without love. For love would be love of the wrong thing. There is yet faith, but the hope, and the love, and the faith are all in the waiting.
T. S. Eliot

Take delight in the Lord, and He will give you the desires of your heart. Commit your way to the Lord; trust in Him and He will act.
Psalms 37:4-5

Faith is not unlike being on a runaway horse. If you take seriously the love of God to be the ultimate motivating power, not just of your life, but of the world, it takes you. You are not in control. But you trust that this wild expression of faith gives you something that is greater than the false illusions of your security systems of the past.
Michael D. Anderson, *This is the Day*

❧4❧

Balance

4ᵀᴴ Rule of the Universe
Every problem in the world,
personal or global, has a
balance issue.

Corollary:
Incremental balancing on
the physical, intellectual,
and spiritual planes brings
exponential results.

*O*sama bin Laden and Hitler are extreme examples of persons whose out-of-balance beliefs caused incomprehensible destruction. Bin Laden, we are told, feels completely justified in causing the destruction of lives and property on September 11th. (I went from dove to hawk as I watched on television the collapse of the Twin Towers when I lived within walking distance of the Pentagon.)

On a personal scale, we have seen wonderfully talented people sabotage their lives by misusing drugs, food, alcohol, sex—even exercise and dieting. Fanaticism and addiction look for satisfaction outside the higher self and always come up empty.

Blinded by ambition? Blinded by radical religious beliefs? In our American view, bin Laden is extremely out of balance but is a hero to those who subscribe to his radical beliefs.

How do we reconcile our own government's military actions? My father and uncle, both pilots in the U.S. Air Force, flew missions in Viet Nam. If they were still alive, they would say that one purpose of our country's fighting was and is to liberate enslaved people from barbaric political and social laws. Huge difference. My cousin Bill Looney, who is a USAF four-star general, is carrying on the family tradition.

Are we blinded by our ambition to get ahead, to climb that social ladder to "Emptyville," to create a perfect world with perfect friends, to crown our egos king or queen of the universe?

This is not to say that setting and achieving challenging and even ambitious goals are empty or evil pursuits. Accomplishment can be the highest manifestation of our God-given talents. The question is have we gone overboard in our quest for personal success? Consider the notorious example of the ice-skater Tonya Harding:

blinded by ambition, she lost all sense of balance (no pun intended) and hired a man to maim her competitor, Nancy Kerrigan.

Why do we get out of balance? Are we trying to anesthetize ourselves to pain, loss, fear, or even our own power and success? Going through my second divorce, I burned the candle at both ends—during the day, learning oil and gas law on the job; in the evenings, drinking wine and not eating.

I became anemic; although I felt so bad at the time I thought I had a much more serious problem. My blood sugar levels were so out of whack that, once I was on the mend, I craved hamburgers every three hours and would go nuts if I didn't eat them on schedule. My friends and family were very patient with me as I began to balance myself.

During this time, my second divorce in four years, I started using affirmations, which can be amazingly effective tools. They plant seeds in our subconscious and conscious minds that can change our behavior with surprising ease.

Writing out positive statements about

yourself can work wonders. In those days of self-doubt, fear, and desperate financial need, affirmations such as these helped me: "Every day I am calmer and calmer." (I was in a panic state.) "Everyday I am more and more healthy." (I was a physical wreck.) "Everyday I recognize my true value." (My self-esteem was at an all time low.) "Everyday God will reveal His plan for my life." (And He did! I went into oil and gas law, one year later was hired by an excellent corporation, and joyfully moved from Oklahoma City, where the two divorces had made a see-saw out of my life, to "the Big D"—Dallas.)

At the base of our out-of-balance behavior is fear. We feel down deep that we won't have our needs met, won't achieve what we want, aren't good enough, smart enough, on and on. So we try to alter our state—with a glass of wine that becomes a bottle, a hit of grass that becomes a baggie, a slice of bread that becomes a loaf, a pair of shoes that becomes a closet. And we don't come up empty; we come up stuffed with toxins, guilt, bills, and self-loathing.

All because we lacked faith in the universe

that our heart's desires would come to us. We over-schedule our calendars and over-feed our bodies to fill our emotions. Eckhart Tolle's *The Power of Now* and Gary Zukav's *The Seat of the Soul* take in-depth looks at how our addictions and cravings, judgments and lack of forgiveness, keep us from realizing our heart's desires and soul's purpose by looking outside ourselves for fulfillment.

The cure is not discipline. The cure is to start dreaming, really dreaming, visualizing ourselves the way we want to be, believing in ourselves as divine creations with miraculous talents.

Rather than bore you by telling you how I try to give up chocolate and lose the eternal ten pounds, I'm going to paraphrase Stephen Covey's story on balance. A woman is out in her field furiously but unsuccessfully sawing wood. Her neighbor comes up and asks what she is doing. "Can't you see? I am sawing wood." Her neighbor says, "Well, why don't you sharpen your saw? It will go so much faster." The woman exclaims, "I don't have time!" Stephen Covey is telling us that when we sharpen our saw in the physical, intellectual, and spiritual areas of our lives, everything goes better for us. When we devote incremental effort to a balanced life, we realize exponential results and growth.

Even if our efforts of attention seem for years to be producing no result, one day a light that is in exact proportion to them will flood the soul.
Simone Weil

The good news is we have the power to balance the competing forces in our lives on the physical, intellectual, and spiritual planes.

How do we use that power to break an out-of-balance cycle? Writing down our present (out-of-balance) states and then where we want to be helps tremendously. This exercise gets us focused on what we want (to be balanced) and separates us from what we don't want (to be out of control). Sometimes we need divine intervention, which can even come through the help of friends. Going on a walk, reading a great book, watching a good film, or meditating on a spiritual quotation helps me restore my sense of balance.

Andrew Weil's approach is also helpful. In his book, *Eight Weeks to Optimum Health*, he suggests walking just ten minutes a day, gradually increasing to an hour a day. Likewise, in trying to change our eating habits, he suggests that we start by substituting one healthy meal for an unhealthy one and keep changing the equation until we are eating mostly healthy meals.

Breaking down my day into units and then scheduling as many healthy/productive units as possible is what works for me. I'm not a cold turkey kind of person. Tell me I can't have something (such as chocolate) and it's the only thing I can think about. When it comes to wine, I take the first glass of wine, the wine takes the second glass, and then the wine takes me.

So when I am really serious about balancing on the physical plane (I quit using the word "diet"), I forgo my favorite red wine. I know when I am eating and drinking in a healthy, balanced way and when I am not, when I am feeding my emotions rather than my body. And I don't have to tell you when I feel my best.

Physical balancing often gets more attention

than intellectual or spiritual balancing, perhaps because its results are more obvious. Certainly being out of balance physically can affect our minds. Not eating and exercising properly can cause depression, irritability, and a sense of hopelessness. Too much sugar and not enough protein and exercise and I'm one step away from being a serial killer. Many doctors recommend diet and exercise. Yet it seems that much of the medical profession's focus is on prescribing pills to fix a newly discovered malady, the "syndrome du jour."

Intellectual and spiritual balancing is equally critical to our well-being. Obsessive ideas in the religious and spiritual areas are dangerous when people claim God's name to legitimize actions that feed their internal passions. Consider cruelties and injustices, now horrifying to us, committed in the name of Christianity: inquisitions in the Middle Ages, the Salem witch trials in the seventeenth century. That one, in fact, comes close to home. My husband's ancestor, Martha Carrier, was executed by drowning in Salem, Massachusetts because she was falsely accused of being a witch. She also happened to own land that was confiscated after her death by those who prosecuted her case.

There are horrors in the world. Evil is real but not triumphant. When I am analyzing any action or idea, near or far, mine or someone else's, I hold it up to the balance test. Does this action, idea, result, go overboard? Does it cross the line of reason, beauty, safety, good taste? This type of critical thinking is different from judging in a negative way a person or situation. The first one is from a detached and rational perspective; the second one from emotional involvement.

We can't control others but we can make choices and stand up for what we believe is right. It seems the last person we ever dream of controlling is ourselves, and yet "Self" is the only person we can control. If someone wants to control me—a dangerous premise to begin with—the best course of action is to set the example for me, not tell me what to do. As I set examples for others—and all of us do with every action we take—do my actions reflect my values and are my values balanced?

Being out of balance creates all sorts of problems that we then need to deal with. In addition, our frantic, racing thoughts and actions cut us off from universal intelligence and the source of all creation. When, in our hearts, we know we are balancing—bringing equilibrium back to our body, mind, and soul—we feel calm, empowered, and centered.

As the hymn says, "Let there be peace on earth, and let it begin with me." If our faith were strong enough, would we still engage in behavior that is out of balance? If we trusted the universe completely, would we not balance our lives on the physical, intellectual, and spiritual planes?

A PRAYER

Dear God,
In my frantic state
of useless anxiety,
please calm me
with your supreme serenity,
knowing that as a child of God
I can tap into
universal intelligence
when I am quiet,
so quiet I can hear
my eyelashes move.
In my new state
of detached observer,
I will watch for your messages
behind my eyes.

Amen

The Ultimate Cocktail
Daily Affirmations on Balance

Today I stop compulsive behavior;
it never gives me what I seek.

Today I unplug the
seductive deceiver's tempting
rationalizations.

Today I recognize that evil is real
but not triumphant.

Today I break old patterns with
one action that makes a difference.

Today I ask God's help in
bringing balance to all areas of
my life.

Today I celebrate at the ultimate
level above food and drink.

Today my actions reflect my
new thinking.

Additional passages that help me achieve balance:

God has not given us the spirit of fear, but of power, and of love, and a sound mind.
2 Timothy 1:7 RSV

Let go of longing and aversion, and everything will be perfectly clear. With not even a trace of self-doubt, you can trust the universe completely.
All at once you are free, with nothing left to hold onto. All is empty, brilliant, perfect in its own being. Step aside from all thinking, and there is nowhere you can't go.
Returning to the root, you find the meaning; chasing appearances, you lose their source. At the moment of profound insight, you transcend both appearance and emptiness.
Chinese Zen Master Seng-Ts'an,
The Mind of Absolute Trust

❦5❧
Attitude

5ᵗʰ Rule of the Universe
Our attitude toward other
people determines their
attitude toward us.

Corollary:
Gratitude and humor
are the elixirs of life,
diffusing negativity,
enhancing creativity.

*R*obert Altman, my boss at PBS, and Carol Dickert-Scher, the head of Human Resources, as gently as they could, gave me the shocking news that I was part of the reduction-in-force. "It is not a reflection of your performance," they said, "but you are to pack up your office and leave as soon as possible."

I responded, "PBS has been very good to me. And if I were in your place, I would have made the same decision." I knew the logic of business decisions: it made sense to cut a highly paid head of a department that was not a corporate priority of the new CEO.

I am convinced that my attitude in that

meeting led to two events: an interview and a job offer at the National Gallery of Art, and my former PBS boss becoming a donor to the Gallery. It turned out that the HR director at PBS recommended me to her twin sister, Cathie Scoville, who was a major gifts officer for the National Gallery. Cathie introduced me to the Gallery's director of development who subsequently hired me.

Attitude is like postage: the right attitude delivers our hearts' desires. What is within us, we send out to the world, and the world sends it back to us while we remain convinced "reality" is something concrete outside of us. As in quantum physics, the observer *and* the instruments of measurement used to observe have an effect on what is seen and experienced. We see reality through the lenses of our human eyes.

The real voyage of discovery consists not in seeking new landscapes, but in having new eyes.
Marcel Proust

In *Codependent No More,* Melody Beattie explains the transformative effect that the attitude of gratitude has on our lives. Being grateful turns everything around. Gratitude, she said, makes a home out of a house, a feast out of a meal, a friend out of a stranger. To appreciate, rather than criticize, what we have before us changes our experience of life for the good.

We have so much to be grateful for: to live in a free society where we can earn our own living and where health care is reasonably available. At closer range, a walk through a cancer center reception room where bald patients wait for their chemotherapy treatment puts superficial issues into perspective.

Even if you find yourself to be one of those patients, your prognosis will be much better if you approach your ordeal with a positive and hopeful attitude. My good friend Emily DeCicco is fighting stomach cancer with incredible bravery, humor, and style. Emily and her devoted husband, Frank, who is a physician, threw a fabulous party after Emily's first round of chemotherapy. "I plan parties, not funerals,"

Emily told me in an upbeat tone on the phone. Two hundred friends and family members from all over the country came to support Emily and Frank.

In her elegant black turban (her hair fell out the day before the party), Emily was the belle of the ball and you would never know she was facing a life-threatening disease. Everyone danced, told stories, and marveled at Emily and Frank's courage. The example they are setting with their attitude puts them at the top of the list of people I most admire in the world.

Emily called me the evening following her third round of chemotherapy to say that the results of her latest tests were encouraging. "We're not out of the woods yet, but we're moving in the right direction. I'm still running the mayoral race for a Washington, D.C. candidate but I am fatigued."

I said, "So now you just have the energy level of a normal person. I bet Georgetown Hospital will never be the same." "Well, all the interns are following the mayoral race for the first time!" she chirped.

Books abound on the benefit of laughter and humor in helping the human body heal, reducing stress, and promoting happiness. Whether we are going through cancer treatment or just dealing with the nitty-gritty of daily life, our sense of humor can be our best companion.

If we really believe in the Resurrection, that we have life everlasting, wouldn't we entertain a sense of humor most of the time? Humor does more to diffuse difficult or awkward situations than all the philosophy in the world. Like faith, humor lives in the incongruous, in the illogical. And we all love to be around those who have a sense of humor.

Sometimes putting ourselves in the right frame of mind requires a few mind games. Motivational speaker Anthony Robbins suggests that, when facing a situation or task we are dreading, we ask ourselves: "What would make this fun for me? How can I *make* this fun?" One of his examples was to relax in the comfort of a hot tub when you need to make a dozen phone calls.

I ask myself "What is good about this?" in situations where I could easily become irritated.

Here's a mundane example of a time when good came from something that I didn't want to happen. After having guests over for dinner, I could not find one of my engraved sterling silver place spoons. I am sure that it found its way to the trash as we cleared the table and cleaned up the kitchen. I could have ordered a replacement from Neiman-Marcus but thinking of the cost made me irritable.

Out shopping one day, I chanced upon an antique store that had a silver consignment section. I didn't find a spoon like the one I lost, but I did find some lovely spoons that work with my pattern, plus a very special serving piece, all for a fraction of their original cost.

If I had not lost my place spoon I would not have added (at a bargain) some beautiful pieces to my silver collection. If I had not been laid off at PBS, I would not have worked at the National Gallery of Art. If my prior marriages had not ended in divorce, I would not be married now to the man who is perfect for me.

Just when we think we've got it made, however, we get yet another unacceptable circumstance. Joyce Meyer said, "When you go to the next level, you get a new devil." Here I am married to the love of my life, and I am diagnosed with apnea. This disorder causes me to stop breathing while I'm asleep resulting in loud snoring and jerky motions. Doesn't that sound sexy?

When I was at the sleep clinic, I cried through the mask that covered my face. I could not fall asleep that first night and had to check into the sleep clinic once again to endure another miserable night in that strange place with wires taped all over my body.

My father's fatal heart attack very possibly could have been caused by apnea although his condition was never diagnosed. I faked an attitude of gratitude—"Good thing we know this; it could save my life." Underneath that façade, I was mad.

After one week of looking like Darth Vader in the bedroom, I checked the Internet for alternatives to wearing the full-face mask that left indentations on my face until noon and was, in my opinion, better suited for firefighters. I found breathing tubes that were much better, especially after I replaced the stiff black straps with soft material and colorful ponytail bands.

When I think of the classmates and colleagues I have known that had severe physical problems, it makes my attitude toward the breathing machine pretty lame. In the sixth grade, I had a friend named Cheryl who was born unable to move her arms or hands. She wore a brace around her torso that attached to braces on her arms and hands.

To write she swung her braced arm around from her side and dropped her little finger on her electric typewriter, one key at a time. It was a slow and laborious process. I helped Cheryl with her underwear when she needed to go the bathroom. I never heard her complain or saw her pleasant face in a frown. We moved to another state and I never saw or spoke to Cheryl after that year but her remarkable attitude left a lasting impression.

I work at responding to life's situations with a good attitude (in most cases), but I was blessed from the start with a happy disposition.

It might be easier for me than for others to look at things in a positive light just as it is easier for others to play tennis or golf.

No matter where we start, we have all been given free choice, and it is up to us to choose how we interpret situations in our lives. Denis Waitley's advice, "Do within when you're without," has more than once pulled me out of a funk in those "parched and barren" times in my life, or given me a little more self-discipline when I needed to cut back.

Counselor Jim Hays told me, "We can make our salads every day with the fresh ingredients always before us, or we can go the garbage of the past with predictable results." Letting our past dictate our present or constantly judging separates us from the joys and miracles that surround us.

Not that we are supposed to be a superficial version of Pollyanna in a fairy-tale world letting everything roll off our backs. My response to some events in my life is anger and resolve. In my last year of college I dated a talented writer whom I had known in high school. We had talked about getting married when he returned from Vietnam. By then I had graduated from college and was working as a bank teller in Oklahoma City. I had put on the standard 20 pounds at school.

When Thom saw the fat me, the marriage plans evaporated. The anger I felt was good. My *modus operandi* became, "I will make myself acceptable to *you*, and then I will reject you." I quit my job at the bank and took a waitress job at an upscale restaurant at the suggestion of my mother. I rented my first apartment with my new friend, Jackie Sparkes, whom I had met at the restaurant. I lost the extra 20 pounds, and then some. Thinner than I had been in years, I felt great, made new friends, and fell in love.

I have applied that same *m.o.* at other times in my life when I have been rejected. I resolve to go beyond the standards on which my rejector judged me. This *m.o.* has driven me to achieve things I might not have otherwise. I refuse to be diminished. Throw me out the window, cat-like, I land on my feet.

I was blessed to know the late Barth Walker.

He was a mentor to me and many others. Barth was born in Arkansas and raised by "ladies of the night" whom he spoke of with affection and appreciation. He didn't have a lick of money, but he had faith, determination, and a willingness to work hard. Football was his ticket to the University of Oklahoma. Then he put himself through law school.

Barth never wasted a second feeling sorry for himself or embarrassed by his humble background. He was not just a successful lawyer. He was highly respected and known in Oklahoma as the "father of oil and gas law." He was a Sunday school teacher and friend.

The phrase "he has a chip on his shoulder" would never be used to describe this man. We have all worked with individuals that phrase perfectly describes who started life with a lot more than Barth Walker did. I was sad when Barth died but he lived a full life. He never acted his age (91 years old) or his status (a multi-millionaire). His obituary began, "What do you say about a giant of a man who was 5 feet 6 inches tall?"

When we find ourselves feeling like "clods

of ailments and grievances complaining that the world does not devote itself to making us happy" as George Bernard Shaw described, we need to start the blessing countdown. Thank God you're not in prison. (If you're not.) Thank God you're not in the hospital. (If you're not.) Take a deep breath and thank God you can breathe without pain. (If you can.) Thank God you can move without pain. (If you can.) Thank God you don't have to go to court. (If you don't.) Thank God you have parents, however crazy they may be. (If you do.) Thank God you had parents you knew. (If you did.) Thank God you are alive. (I think we are on safe ground here.) And if that doesn't work, read the rest of this book.

A P R A Y E R

Dear Lord of all Creation,
Before whom all is as dust and a vapor,
may I stay tuned to your infinite power
to forgive, to heal, to love, to laugh.
In Jesus' name we pray.

Amen

The Ultimate Cocktail
Daily Affirmations on Attitude

Today I thank God for all the lessons He has given me.

Today I welcome new learning and new loving.

Today I leave the past behind and create my life with a clean slate.

Today I ask myself, how can I make this task/situation fun?

Today I dress up to meet my destiny and greet the day with hope.

Today I respond to life with humor and joy.

Today my feelings of gratitude bring peace, hope, and love.

Additional passages to help my attitude:

The longer I live, the more I realize the impact of attitude on life.

Attitude, to me, is more important than the past, than education, than money, than circumstances, than failures, than success, than what other people think or say or do.

It is more important than appearance, giftedness or skill. It will make or break an organization, a school, a home.

The remarkable thing is we have a choice every day regarding the attitude we will embrace for that day.

We cannot change our past. We cannot change the fact that people will act in a certain way. We cannot change the inevitable.

The only thing we can do is play the one string we have. And that is our attitude. I am convinced that life is 10 percent what happens to me and 90 percent how I react to it. And so it is with you.

Charles Swindell

What is before us and behind us are tiny matters compared to what is within us.

Oliver Wendell Holmes

❧6☙
Priorities

6ᵀᴴ Rule of the Universe
When we focus on our
highest values and goals,
trivialities vanish.

Corollary:
Simplicity is a luxury;
less is more.

*A*merican culture seduces us into thinking that we should do everything and have everything. Or, at least, die trying. We are bombarded by information and choices. We have more material things than we can use. We run ourselves ragged with our kinetic appointment calendars and to-do lists. We think we're going to miss something if we don't leave all our options open. And we indeed are missing something: a life well-lived.

On my bathroom wall is a clock that says, "There is always enough time for the important things in life." What is important in my life? Relationships are at the top for me—my relationship to God, to my husband, my family and friends. And my relationship to myself.

I did not always put God first, as I explained

in chapter three. (And lest I sound saint-like, keeping God top-of-mind is a continual struggle—just like keeping negative thoughts out-of-mind.) As far as human relationships, I remember the many times in my past when I thought that declaring truth and direction for all the world was the measure of a sophisticated, discerning person.

My friend Helen Manich, a successful businesswoman, taught me this insightful wisdom about relationships, "You are either right or you are in relationship." She means that we choose to win arguments or to be in a relationship. If we really want the relationship, we aren't concerned about being "right." We are quick to bicker about the small stuff while a wonderland whirls around us. (This is different from "peace at any price.") How many relationships implode because each person insists on his or her way?

Out beyond all notions of right and wrong, there is a field. I will meet you there.
Jelaluddin Rumi

Helen Manich also told me: "Other people's behavior is 100 percent about them and zero percent about you. Your behavior is 100 percent about you and zero percent about other people." Now that is personal accountability! The way someone treats us speaks volumes about that person. Our response to someone else's behavior is our total responsibility. No one *makes* us feel one way or another; no one *makes* us do one thing over another. People can do things that are hurtful but we are in charge of how we respond.

The relationship to myself is a reflection of my relationship to God and to my loved ones. I can't be patient and loving to others when my mind and body are screaming at me because I haven't taken proper care of them. The body is the temple of the soul but do we honor the miracle of the human body?

Or do we treat our bodies like Cinderella's step sisters treated her: make her work hard, ignore her needs, and then complain about her? When I devote time to balancing on the physical, intellectual, and spiritual planes, discussed in chapter four, all my relationships benefit.

Life-long learning, whether formal learning in institutions or reading and learning on our own, is one of the best presents we can give ourselves and is second on my list of priorities. Better than diamonds, life-long learning *is* the gift that keeps on giving.

Learning enhances another of my priorities—creativity. Using our minds and hearts to create something—whether it is a meal, a book, a song, a building, whatever—puts us in touch with the essence of the universe. Totally absorbed in a creative endeavor can transform our grief and hopelessness to joy and purpose.

To prepare ourselves for our relationships, learning, and creativity, we need to do two things: seek solitude and practice simplicity.

Solitude is good for us in every way imaginable. We can center ourselves, get in touch with our Creator, listen for God's messages, and give our minds a rest from daily distractions. Books like Sarah Ban Breathnach's *Simple Abundance* and Deepak Chopra's *The Seven Spiritual Laws of Success* are two of my favorite resources for bringing me back to the practice of solitude.

Solitude is also how we access that magical field, so many writers describe, from which we can create most anything we want. Deepak Chopra uses the example of throwing a stone into a still pond and watching the ripples it creates. The stone is a desire or intention. We are the pond. If we are as still as a glassy pond, the stone (our intention) can connect to this universal energy field and help us realize our desires. If we are like a turbulent ocean, we can throw a dozen stones in but nothing happens. Or to use another analogy, we can't send a fax (our intention) when we are talking on the same phone line.

In order to have solitude and peace, we may need to simplify our lives. Too much "stuff" gets in the way. Don't we love the feeling we have after cleaning out a closet? In spite of knowing how good it will feel, we engage in all sorts of distractions and displacement activity to avoid getting rid of things we don't use.

I kept things for years, never using them,

paying to store them, paying to move them, and then one day decided to give those things away, and presto, I felt lighter. I carried around my heavy law books for years thinking that one day I would actually read them. Or maybe my ego thought that they would look impressive in my bookcase. How ridiculous is that?

Let go, whether it is old books we don't treasure or use, clothes we do not wear, or myriad things around the house that someone else might actually use. Let go! Saving all these things, hoarding them in case you *might* need them shows a mentality of lack, not abundance, and the universe will respond accordingly. When you are holding on, you are telling the universe: *I may need; I won't have (the money to replace this).* The universe listens and gives you what you say to yourself.

Jane Campion's film, *The Piano*, portrays a heroine who insists that her beloved piano, her obsession, be thrown into the sea so that she can be free of her past and start a new life. We wonder why our lives don't change yet we hold on to the old one through all the material props that created it. Changing what surrounds the outside of us helps change what's inside.

Simplicity is a luxury that everyone can enjoy. "You can't have everything. Where would you put it?" posits comedian Stephen Wright. Why *do* we want so much in the first place? Adding beautiful things to our surroundings can be a healthy celebration of life but how quickly we can become obsessive in wanting more, more, more of everything we don't need.

William Wordsworth, writing in 1807, offered words worth a lot today: "The world is too much with us; late and soon, Getting and spending, we lay waste our powers." We live in a society that values material wealth but think of the people you know who have all the money in the world and yet are not happy or fulfilled.

Having spent 15 years in fundraising, I was fascinated (and sometimes disappointed) to learn how generous some multi-millionaires were and how some were not. One of my early lessons in this was from two Mary Baldwin College alumnae. One I visited in her unpretentious home. This refined, older woman loved that college. Documenting the visit, as fundraisers do, I wrote in my report that I thought she would be a good annual fund supporter (that is, give smaller gifts regularly) but that she was not a candidate for a major gift. After I circulated my report to all of my colleagues, I learned she had sent the college a check for $80,000.

The other alumna picked me up at the airport in her new red Mercedes convertible, took me to one of the fanciest restaurants in town, and told me all about her trips to Africa and Europe. I knew that she was on her pricey city's Best Dressed list. Her gift to the college? $250.

I learned that a person with a rusty Chevrolet in her driveway could make a legacy gift. She had different priorities for spending her money.

Relationships, learning, creativity, solitude, and simplicity—what do these have in common? They take me outside of my ego and put me in touch with the living God and the divinity within me. In my husband's book, *The Scent of Life, A Pocket Prayer Book for the Discovery of Life*, I found this prayer:

I cannot hear you when I am listening to the fear-filled voice of my inner consciousness. I cannot hear you when superficial material needs nag me for attention. Hearing, you have taught me, comes first from silence. 'Be still and know that I am God,' is the simple instruction you have given.

Isn't that all we need?

THE ULTIMATE COCKTAIL
DAILY AFFIRMATIONS ON PRIORITIES

Today I appreciate what I have instead of valuing what I don't have.

Today I put people above things, relationships above being right.

Today I follow through on my promises to others and myself.

Today I finish what yesterday's procrastination left undone.

Today I practice the luxury of simplicity.

Today I calm myself and listen in deep silence.

Today my values direct my everyday living.

Additional passages that help me prioritize:

If you don't know how to spend an entire day doing absolutely nothing, then you don't know how to live.
Gertrude Stein

Seek first the kingdom of God and God's righteousness; and all these things shall be added unto you.
Matthew 6:33 KJV

I'm erecting a barrier of simplicity between myself and the world.
André Gide

❧ 7 ❧

Illusions & Dreams

7ᵀᴴ RULE OF THE UNIVERSE
Illusions are thoughts we have about
the world that do not work.

When we let go of illusions and face
the truth, our internal conflict ceases.

"Facts" are perceptions about ourselves
that limit us. When we ignore the
"facts," our dreams rush to meet us.

*H*ave you ever been in a relationship that you deeply desired, but the more you tried to make it work, the more painful it was for you? If we are experiencing psychological pain about a situation, that is a clue that we may be letting our ego drive rather than our higher self.

I would date a man I *thought* was perfect for me but then there was a long list of things that he needed to do before this "perfect match" brought the happiness I expected. I call this the Prince Charming syndrome. That person you think is a prince might be a frog. Better let go of him before you get warts.

When we force things in a personal relationship or in a business setting, or when we are forcing ourselves to be something that does not come from within, we are checking into heartbreak hotel.

In my last week of work at the University of Virginia Law School Foundation before heading to Washington, D.C. to work for PBS, a visiting alumnus walked up to me during alumni weekend and said, "I bet you're not from Virginia." His comment started a relationship that would carry me through my breast cancer treatment.

David had just stepped off the airplane from Los Angeles for a weekend visit when I told him I was having a little procedure (the lumpectomy) the upcoming Monday and that if he wanted to get on a plane back to L.A. I would understand. He canceled his entire week of appointments, not an easy thing to do for a lawyer with his own practice, and stayed the long week until the pathology report came back. He kept me laughing the entire time. "Where do you want to go for your last supper?" he asked the night before the operation.

I was shocked when David took me to the cancer section of a bookstore. I was in denial. "I just have a tiny malignant tumor that I'm going to get rid of," I said to myself. I couldn't even use the "C" word.

Afterward when it was evident I had no symmetry to my bodice, he said, "I'll build up one side of my body, and we'll be known as the Asymmetrical Couple." (Many women have lumpectomies, losing so little breast tissue that symmetry is not an issue.) David Farrar and I would not have a long-term relationship, but he was a Godsend who led me as I stepped through the breast cancer minefield.

My mother and my friends could not have been more giving throughout this time. Gail Haynes, my closest friend, did what she always does: assesses your needs quickly and rushes to meet them along with flowers, champagne, and beautifully wrapped gifts. She flew in from Connecticut for the mastectomy and reconstructive surgeries, made sure the doctors were taking proper care of me, and laughed with my mother—so much so they were late picking me up from the hospital! Marie Kimmel helped me move into my new apartment one week after my last surgery when I could not even pick up a bath towel. Skipper Jones made me a card that said, "Cancer is so limited," brought me baskets of goodies, and took me to a spiritual retreat at the National Cathedral. Connie Ingles called me from White Marsh every day for months. Dr. Frank DeCicco went with me for my first biopsy.

Still it was psychologically comforting to have a man's affection in the midst of losing a body part that in our culture symbolizes a woman's desirability. David also introduced me to breast cancer survivors who helped me make the irreversible decisions I had to make.

One of the most valuable lessons I learned throughout the breast cancer treatment—eight months of tests, surgeries, needles and more needles—was that we must manage our own health. We cannot turn over our lives and physical well-being to an all-knowing doctor. Each of us is in charge of our body. Trying to decide whether to have a mastectomy (or live the rest of my life noticeably asymmetrical), and then to decide what kind of reconstructive surgery among several options, was incredibly stressful for me. None of the seven doctors I had to consult could tell me what was best for me. It was solely my decision. Talking to women who had faced those same decisions made a big difference.

Help shows up all the time, although sometimes we don't recognize it. We want to put the gifts we receive in our own boxes using our own labels. Labels on relationships aren't any more useful than labels on women's clothing that irritate and show through.

Illusions cause enormous pain. Letting go of illusions and facing the truth about a situation or relationship brings almost instant peace. I was looking for a permanent relationship when the purpose of that particular relationship was to help me face the fact that I had cancer and to support me emotionally through the surgeries.

Letting go of illusions and facing the truth is always a good idea. An Alexandria, Virginia, therapist who counseled me regarding my breast cancer and relationship issues said to me, "When are you going to quit attracting emotionally unavailable men like your father?" I protested.

Daddy had died years before and I wanted to preserve my memory of him as a perfect person. What I still needed to do was look at my relationship to men as a continuation of the unresolved relationship to my father. Daddy was available to me for anything and everything I needed, but we did not have conversations about my (or his) feelings.

I needed to forgive my father for not being perfect. Then I could love him completely as my handsome, hard-working, smart, talented, and loving father who loved me and showed it the best way he knew how.

When we face the truth, we can quit running away. We carry around emotional baggage for years afraid to open the steamer trunk, afraid of what we will discover. Our discoveries heal us so that we can become healthy, balanced persons capable of healthy relationships.

Truth is not the same as "facts," which are perceptions about ourselves that limit us. People who realize their dreams ignore "facts" (all the limitations that discourage them) and stay focused on their goals. In *An Open Book*, Ruth Gordon cautioned, "Don't face facts." Ms. Gordon dreamed of starring on Broadway. Family, teachers, friends, and acquaintances tried to discourage her. She was told she lacked talent, beauty, money, and connections. She ignored "facts" and never stopped dreaming. Well into her 80s, her full career of acting, on Broadway and in film, won her an Oscar and endeared her to millions of fans. If successful people listened to what other people told them, none would have reached their goals.

Risk! Risk anything! Care no more for the opinions of others, for those voices. Do the hardest thing on earth for you. Act for yourself. Face the truth.
Katherine Mansfield

Sometimes we have to change careers to follow our dreams, our callings. We are faced with the dilemma of not wanting to face the unknown (or lack of steady income) but feel compelled to make the change. If we're lucky, our callings won't let us alone. They will sabotage our status quo to jolt us out of our familiar yet off-purpose routines. Getting a signal from the universe is sometimes the best thing that can happen.

My fundraising career was rewarding and was my calling for 15 years. Now I am on to another adventure, a calling that now resonates much deeper and stronger than fundraising—writing. I am trusting that the net will appear as I leap into this unknown territory.

I dreamed of going to Paris with no means to do so. I dreamed of success in my fundraising career. I dreamed of marrying someone perfectly suited to me—all these dreams I put on my magic refrigerator and they came true.

My heart's desire now is being published and having a book signing at the Paris Ritz. To realize those desires, I have to do what I did before— "don't face facts" and dream my dream.

Now let me tell you how my magic refrigerator sent me to Paris free. This is a story about ignoring "facts" and focusing on my heart's desires.

It all started when I lived in the beautiful Shenandoah Valley of Virginia. My next-door neighbors, Allen and Gary, were going to Paris and I asked them to send me a postcard of I.M. Pei's pyramid entrance at the Louvre.

The moment the postcard arrived, I put it on my refrigerator and said, "I want to go to Paris. I really want to go to Paris." Every time I opened the refrigerator, I repeated my deep desire. I could not afford a trip to the City of Lights. I didn't know anyone in Paris nor did I speak the language. In the middle of a divorce, not making much money, "facts" rendered this dream impossible.

Then something magical happened.

Travel agents from Intrav, a St. Louis company, did business with Mary Baldwin College, where I was working. They took me to lunch to work the account. Over lunch I jokingly said to them, "If you ever have an extra seat on a plane to Paris, I need to go."

One year later, to my amazement, they called and asked, "Do you still want to go to Paris? We have a group going from North Carolina and from the University of Michigan, and there's an extra seat that's already paid for."

So there I was in September of 1994 touring France, visiting Versailles, Monet's Giverny, and all of Paris, the City of Lights. I stood in front of I.M. Pei's La Pyramide du Louvre, the picture on the postcard on my refrigerator back in Virginia. The only money I had to spend was the "walking around money" that my dear friend Gail had sent me. And, for the return trip to the United States, we flew on the supersonic Concorde. All free. That was the beginning of my magic refrigerator.

I started posting other "dreams" on my refrigerator. The salary for the job I landed at the University of Virginia Law School Foundation in Charlottesville matched exactly the figure I posted on my refrigerator.

I worked at the Law School Foundation for three years and it was the most rewarding job of my fundraising career. The faculty, staff, and alumni of UVA Law School are great to work with, but I wasn't married or young enough to be happy in Charlottesville. I used to say, "The only dates I ever have are those dark, chewy fruits from the grocery store."

So when I was ready to make a move, I stuck another note on my refrigerator showing the salary and the city (Washington, D.C.) I wanted. A few months later the Public Broadcasting Service in Alexandria, Virginia, offered me a job with the six-figure compensation package I had posted.

My magic refrigerator worked wonders in the professional/financial part of my life, but where's that man in my life? Well, I have to admit I had never put that relationship first.

After my bout with breast cancer, I vowed to go to Italy. I put a small calendar with Italian images on my refrigerator. Sometime later I got a call from my good friend, Caroline McNiece, who told me she was going to be in Italy for ten days by herself because the person she was traveling with, another old friend, Linda Duncan, had to cancel. That trip wasn't free, but Caroline and I had a fabulous time staying in convents in Florence and Todi, and after that a fancy hotel in Rome. I drove on the Autostrada just like the other crazy drivers.

When we were in Florence, I bought a refrigerator magnet of Michelangelo's statue of *David*. Back at home, I put that to use immediately, saying prayerfully there in the kitchen, "God, you know I need a man." That was December 2000 while I was still working at PBS.

By June of the following year, I had called my old church in Oklahoma City for more of the taped sermons I had ordered through the years. (I mentioned this in chapter one.) I did as Linda Ferguson, the church secretary, suggested and called the retired minister to say how sorry I was to hear that his wife had died. I left a voice message.

A few weeks later the minister called to thank me for my message. I told him how much I loved his sermons and that my favorite was "Cool, Clear Water." He said that sermon was in a book of his sermons his daughter Laura had put together. He said he would send me the book.

When I received his book, *This is the Day*, I

flipped immediately to the "Cool, Clear Water" chapter. This was not the text of my favorite sermon. So I called him and told him he had stolen the title. "I can't steal from myself," he laughingly responded. We chatted a bit and I closed with, "If you happen to be in Washington, please let me take you to dinner."

Four months later this man called to say he was coming to Washington for a board meeting at the National Institutes of Health. I again extended my invitation for dinner. I was working at the National Gallery of Art by then and we agreed to meet on the front steps. I was tired that weekend and thought of canceling but I thought that poor man shouldn't have dinner by himself having lost his wife of 44 years.

It was on a Sunday in October and still very warm in D.C. A man gets out of a cab—I hadn't been to Oklahoma City for some time so I wasn't sure this was the minister. He looks different, I thought, but yes...okay, "Hi!" (Later he told me he wondered if he would recognize the person he was meeting—me.) He had a jacket hooked on his fingers over his shoulder, but his shirt was short-sleeved.

I said to myself, "He came to Washington, D.C. and the National Gallery of Art on a *Sunday* in a short-sleeve shirt?" Then I said to myself, "Oh, those *arms*." Minister. *Man*. I had always seen him in a long black robe in church. After a tour of the Gallery and dinner, I tried to give him my business card but he refused to take it. "I'll just lose it," he said.

A year later we were engaged. My husband's name is *Michael David* Anderson and he is my guardian angel. The refrigerator magnet of Michelangelo's *David* worked!

~Conclusion~

The sequence of the 7 Rules is the result of long and careful reflection. In my first manuscript, the first rule was Thought because every action begins with a thought, even the act of faith. In the process of writing, I concluded that before we can think purposefully we must first clear our mind of distracting emotions and so, Acceptance became the first rule, then Thought followed.

Faith appears as the third rule not to signify that it is in third place in the ultimate priorities of life, but that we come to faith through a process of acceptance, a humble spirit, and the right thoughts.

Balance on the physical, intellectual, and spiritual planes as the fourth rule acts as a fulcrum to the remaining three rules. Without balance in our emotions (acceptance), thought, and faith, our attitude, priorities, illusions and dreams will be out of balance in direct proportion.

Attitude, the fifth rule, is our response to what happens to us in life. Responding with humor and gratitude helps in every situation.

The sixth rule, Priorities, redirects us to what we value most: loving, learning, quality over quantity.

The seventh rule, Illusions and Dreams, brings us back to the beginning. Accepting the unacceptable, the first rule, is letting go of illusions in that we release constructs in our mind that impede our growth and happiness. Ignoring "facts," or limitations, and focusing, laser-like, on our dreams, as in the second rule, Thought, bring our dreams to fruition. In the process of analysis, I dissect something that in essence is one phenomenon.

Why seven rules? There are heaps of sevens in our culture from the time of the Biblical creation story in Genesis to our seven days of the week, the Seven Wonders of the World, Snow White and the Seven Dwarfs, the soft drink 7-Up, and the fashionable Seventh Avenue in New York, just to name a few. There is nothing magical about the number 'seven' in my 7 Rules.

What is magical about the 7 Rules is this: by following them, dreams come true. It happened for me and it can happen for you. My dreams are still coming true. Not because I discovered some new magic formula or new secret of the universe. The wisdom contained in the 7 Rules is universal and following it set me free to discover a new reality. That new reality started making a transformative difference in my life.

I used to think that my thoughts were in a self-contained private world separate from what I saw outside of my body. Now I know that my thoughts are like e-mails that I send to the universe. What I send out determines what I get back.

One reason I wanted to write this book is that I wanted to convey to my nephew and niece, my family's only descendants, the ideas and beliefs that I would stake my life on, ideas and beliefs that I think will most help them as they make their way through life. Sloan and Caity, this is my legacy to you. Follow these 7

Rules and your lives will be enriched beyond your wildest imaginations.

Each of us has a unique path. Each of us is "created for such a time as this," as Esther in the Old Testament is told before she musters the courage to risk her life to save her people.

Today we can choose to be co-artists with God to create the masterpiece we are meant to be. God's the master; we're the piece of work. Or we can choose to wander aimlessly and unfulfilled.

God gives us clues to our purpose through our dreams. Believe in your dreams with your whole being. Let God help you. His design for you exceeds your greatest desires. What you will experience may seem like magic, may seem like a miracle, when you are actually dancing in step to God's song of the universe.

A PRAYER

Dear God,
You know my heart's desires
before I do.
Help me to see and believe
the dream you have for me.
Help me to understand
that every trial and tribulation
prepares me for
my ultimate happiness and purpose.
Fill me today, Lord,
with your infinite joy
that I will pass on to others.

Amen.

THE ULTIMATE COCKTAIL
DAILY AFFIRMATIONS ON ILLUSIONS & DREAMS

Today I let go of my illusions and face the truth.

Today I see clear images of myself in my ideal state.

Today I perform specific actions springing from my life purpose.

Today I ignore limitations— "facts"—and visualize my dreams.

Today I dare to believe in my wildest dream.

Today I form the life I am called to live.

Today my dreams rush to meet me.

Additional passages that help me let go of illusions, face the truth, ignore "facts" and dream my dream:

In fact, were it given to our eye of flesh to see into the consciousness of others, we should judge a man [or woman] much more surely from what he [or she] dreams than from what he [or she] thinks.
Victor Hugo, *Les Miserables*

He set my feet upon a rock, making my steps secure, he put a new song in my mouth.
Psalm 40:2-3 RSV

Today your kingdom comes into my midst. My work becomes a calling, my fears are absorbed into love, and my nightmares are turned into dreams. My journey in life is not from birth to death; it is from creation to liberation.
Michael D. Anderson, *The Scent of Life, A Pocket Prayer Book for the Discovery of Life*

THE ULTIMATE COCKTAIL
DAILY AFFIRMATIONS

These daily affirmations follow the 7 Rules. It is amazing how affirmations, messages we send ourselves, create positive behavior modification with seemingly little effort. Test them yourself and see.

1. Acceptance
Today I transform my self and world by accepting the unacceptable.

Today I shower forgiveness on everyone including myself.

Today I experience joy instead of judging.

Today I accept people and situations exactly as they are.

Today I look for meaning in pain, suffering, and loss.

Today I believe the truth that I am accepted by God.

Today my heart changes in the mystery and paradox of love.

2. Thought

Today I separate my true mind from foreign thoughts of negativity.

Today I fearlessly focus on my goals and heart's desires.

Today I fill my subconscious mind with abundance and fulfillment.

Today I attract what I desire starting with my thoughts.

Today I tell myself river stories of hope not rut stories of defeat.

Today I commit to my purpose and the universe moves in my favor.

Today my thoughts move me toward the fruition of my goals.

3. Faith

Today I let in God's power to fulfill my heart's desires and purpose.

Today I listen for God's guidance in place of hurrying and worrying.

Today I release attachment to my desires to allow miraculous results.

Today I trust God's strength more than my own.

Today I step back so God can lead the way.

Today I surrender to God's plans that far exceed mine.

Today my spirit rules my mind and body.

4. Balance

Today I stop compulsive behavior; it never gives me what I seek.

Today I unplug the seductive deceiver's tempting rationalizations.

Today I recognize that evil is real but not triumphant.

Today I break old patterns with one action that makes a difference.

Today I ask God's help in bringing balance to all areas of my life.

Today I celebrate at the ultimate level above food and drink.

Today my actions reflect my new thinking.

5. Attitude

Today I thank God for all the lessons He has given me.

Today I welcome new learning and new loving.

Today I leave the past behind and create my life from a clean slate.

Today I ask myself, how can I make this task/ situation fun?

Today I dress up to meet my destiny and greet the day with hope.

Today I respond to life with humor and joy.

Today my feelings of gratitude bring peace, hope, and love.

6. Priorities

Today I appreciate what I have instead of valuing what I don't have.

Today I put people above things, relationships above being right.

Today I follow through on my promises to others and myself.

Today I finish what yesterday's procrastination left undone.

Today I practice the luxury of simplicity.

Today I calm myself and listen in deep silence.

Today my values direct my everyday living.

7. Illusions and Dreams

Today I let go of my illusions and face the truth.

Today I see clear images of myself in my ideal state.

Today I perform specific actions springing from my life purpose.

Today I ignore limitations—"facts"—and visualize my dreams.

Today I dare to believe in my wildest dream.

Today I form the life I am called to live.

Today my dreams rush to meet me.

~Acknowledgments~

My dream of writing and seeing this book in tangible form was first an idea in my head, then my heart's desire, and finally a labor of love.

My early supporters patiently listened or read and reread my rough drafts which I now look back on in horror. I thank these guardian angels from the bottom of my heart.

Mike, darling, your encouragement when you first read the 7 Rules was manna from heaven. Without your brilliance, humor, patience, and support, in all ways imaginable, this dream of mine would not be coming true. As powerful as words are, I truly cannot find words that could adequately thank you and thank God for the blessing you are in my life.

Mimi, Mommy, you have gone beyond the duties of motherhood (again). Thank you for your many suggestions (most of which I used, you see), your editing and rereading *ad infinitum.* I look forward to returning the favor on your book of prayers. Your beauty and strength are my goals.

Merrilee Callen and **Carm Gemberling,** my dear sisters, thank you for the rich experience of growing up with you providing me with endless material for my writing. Carm, thank you for Wallace Wattles' book you gave me years ago.

Connie Ingles, a true *grande dame,* so much of what I am is because of you. I am deeply grateful for your friendship and for being the first person to call me "a writer."

Gail Chapman Haynes, your generosity and unwavering loyalty, your selfless concern and your refusal to settle for less than the best, make you my friend extraordinaire and adopted sister. Your original *Gailspeak* is incomparable.

Skipper Jones, thank you for all the books and tapes on writing, (and all the other things you have given me) and most of all, for our enduring friendship.

Marie Kimmel, my friend indeed, I will be forever grateful for your many thoughtful actions just when I needed help the most.

Caroline McNiece, your artful personalized travel booklets are cherished reminders of Paris, and Italy, and our many good times together.

Kathe Birnbaum, writer, artist, and the queen of cheer and creativity, I greatly appreciate your enthusiastic friendship and encouragement.

Neal Holland Duncan, Southern gentility in Edwardian eccentricity, author of *Baby Soniat, Naked in the Rhododendrons,* and *She Came of Decent People,* being your neighbor and working on your books was a harbinger for both of us.

Ann Kilpatrick, thank you for reading my manuscript, loaning me books, and introducing me to **Susanne Blake,** author of *When Spirit Speaks* and *Ten Commitments for Women.* Both of you helped me see the possible.

Dale Acker, your friendship to the Catching family is a blessing. Thank you for your edits.

Wanda Gilliam, thank you for introducing me to Ann Lacy.

Steve Mettee of Quill Driver Books/Word Dancer Press, and Lois Qualben of Langmarc Publishing, your early encouragement of a first-time author carried me to the next step. Thank you.

Willee Lewis, your delightful book, *Snakes: An Anthology of Serpent Tales* is a treat for readers of all ages. I appreciate your friendship, support, and publishing advice.

Nicole Barr, your last minute edits were pivotal. Thank you for making a difference.

Lou Kerr, a champion of women, I greatly appreciate your encouragment and support.

To my Mary Baldwin College professors:

Marjorie Chambers, you continue to inspire me. Thank you for opening my eyes in philosophy, living, and writing.

Joe Garrison, your love of language and insistence on critical thinking live on in my writing.

Gwen Walsh, thank you for the discipline of dance and the joy of mind/body balancing. I value our long-standing friendship.

Carl Edwards, working as your student assistant was a gift of learning. Thank you for your help. My writer's block is gone.

And to those who have helped me directly with my labor of love:

Matt Goad of Hit Design, your graphic artistry is masterful. Thanks for creating images for my dream and helping me "make it happen."

Genie Addleton, dear friend and editor, I am deeply grateful to you for your tremendous contributions in the editing and rewriting process.

Ann Lacy and **Jim Alexander** of Macedon Publishing, thank you for mentoring me. You have made possible the tangible realization of my dream.

~About the Author~

Laurel "Lolly" Catching Anderson practiced oil and gas law in Oklahoma and Texas before becoming a fundraiser for her alma mater Mary Baldwin College, then the University of Virginia Law School Foundation, the Public Broadcasting Service (PBS), the National Gallery of Art, the National Cowboy & Western Heritage Museum, and her law school alma mater, Oklahoma City University School of Law.

Happily into her third career—writing—she produces a monthly newsletter, *The Spiritual Times*, available free at **www.thespiritualtimes.com**.

Lolly lives with Mike, her husband, and Aussie, an Australian Kelpie who adopted them, on a beautiful lake in Oklahoma.

Please visit **www.thespiritualtimes.com** to order more copies of *How My Magic Refrigerator Sent Me to Paris Free, 7 Rules to Make Dreams Come True.*

Printed in the United States
63519LVS00001B/199-498